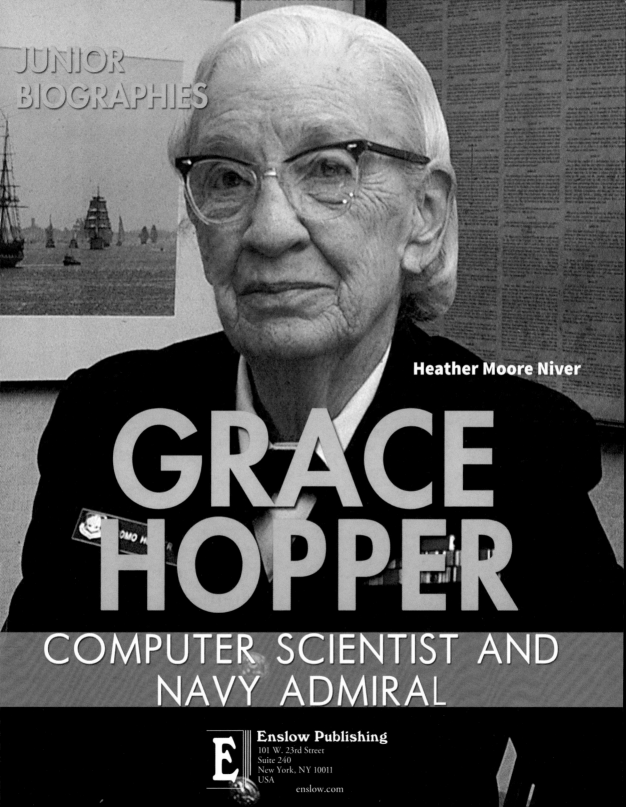

JUNIOR
BIOGRAPHIES

Heather Moore Niver

GRACE HOPPER

COMPUTER SCIENTIST AND NAVY ADMIRAL

Enslow Publishing
101 W. 23rd Street
Suite 240
New York, NY 10011
USA

enslow.com

COBOL A computer language used for business.

computer compiler Software that translates computer codes to different languages.

doctorate The highest degree that is awarded by a college.

electromechanical Describes a mechanical device that is powered by electricity.

mathematician A person who is an expert at math or who is studying math.

physics The science that studies matter, motion, energy, and force.

programmer A person who writes computer programs.

rank A position in an organization.

rear admiral A rank in the US Navy. It is higher than captain and lower than vice admiral.

reserve A nonactive military group. It may be used in an emergency.

CONTENTS

Words to Know 2

Chapter 1 Grace's Girlhood.................... 5

Chapter 2 Mastering the Marks.............. 8

Chapter 3 Computers Are for More
Than Math.............................12

Chapter 4 Back to Active.......................17

Timeline.............................22

Learn More 23

Index 24

Grace Hopper

COMO HOPPER

Rear Admiral Dr. Grace Murray Hopper was not an ordinary mathematician. It's clear from her many nicknames. They include "First Lady of Software" and even "Amazing Grace." Hopper was a genius when it came to math. She also broke new ground in the computer world. She worked on some of the first computers. Her work changed computer technology forever.

A CURIOUS CHILD

Grace Brewster Murray was born on December 9, 1906, in New York City. Her father, Walter, went to Yale University. He owned an insurance company. Grace's mother, Mary

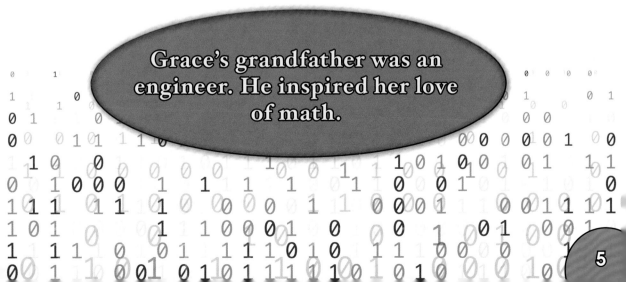

Grace's grandfather was an engineer. He inspired her love of math.

Grace attended Vassar, an all-women's college. This graduation took place at the time Grace was at the school.

Campbell Van Horne, was also a math whiz. Grace was the oldest child. She had a brother named Roger and a sister named Mary.

As a girl, Grace loved to take things apart. When she was only seven, Grace took apart all the clocks in the

house. This was her idea of a good time! She also enjoyed reading. Grace liked to memorize parts of Rudyard Kipling's book *Just So Stories*.

COLLEGE DAYS

Grace was accepted to Vassar College when she was seventeen years old. Her mother was thrilled! Her daughter would have chances that she never had. Grace studied math and physics. She was very good at explaining complicated ideas to other students.

Grace graduated from college in 1928. Two years later, she married Vincent Foster Hopper. He was an English professor. That same year, Grace got another college degree. She also got her doctorate at Yale University in 1934.

Grace Says:

"The most dangerous phrase in the language is, 'We've always done it this way.'"

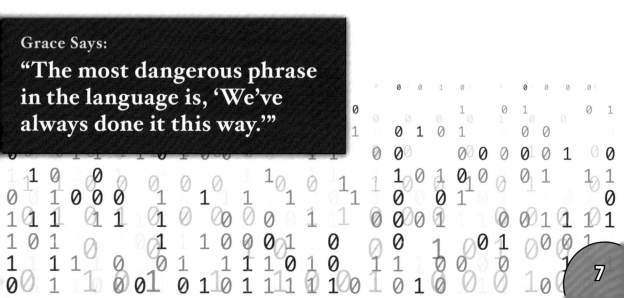

Chapter 2
Mastering the Marks

In 1931, Hopper returned to Vassar. But she was not a student this time. She was a math teacher. She taught for more than ten years. But in 1943, Hopper decided she wanted a change. She wanted to serve her country.

Joining the Navy

The United States had entered World War II. So Hopper joined the US Navy. At first, she was rejected. They said she was too small and too old. But Hopper would not give

Women train for the United States Naval Reserve. The group was better known as WAVES (Women Accepted for Volunteer Emergency Service). Grace joined them in 1943.

up. She joined the US Naval Reserve (Women's Reserve) in December. Hopper was at the top of her training class. She reached the highest training rank there was: battalion commander.

MEETING MARK I

Hopper graduated from training school. She became Lieutenant Grace Hopper. She began working for the Navy and Harvard University. Hopper helped with a special project. It was called the Bureau of Ships Computation Project. She worked with Howard Aiken. He had made one of the first electromechanical computers. It was called the IBM Automatic Sequence Controlled

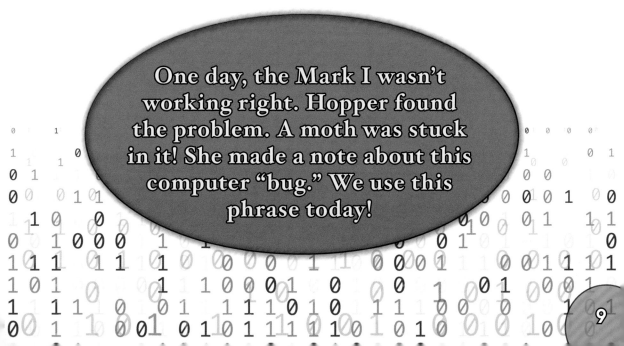

One day, the Mark I wasn't working right. Hopper found the problem. A moth was stuck in it! She made a note about this computer "bug." We use this phrase today!

Calculator. Most people just called it Mark I. When Hopper saw Mark I, she knew she wanted to take it apart. She became one of the first computer programmers.

Not many women worked with computers at this time. Hopper was one of the best in her field. She won an award for her programming on the Mark I, Mark II, and Mark III.

Grace Says:

"Mark I was an impressive beast. She was fifty-one feet long, eight feet high, and five feet deep."

Hopper works at an early computer in 1944.

In 1945, Hopper and her husband got a divorce. They did not have any children. Hopper dated, but she never got married again.

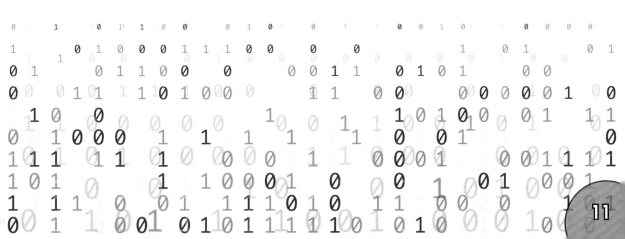

Chapter 3
Computers Are for More Than Math

In 1946, Hopper was turned down for a promotion. The Navy said she was too old. She became part of the Navy reserves. She continued her work on computers. Soon she left Harvard. She would not stay if they would not promote her.

In 1949, Hopper went to Philadelphia. There she started a new job. She worked as a senior mathematician for a computer company. Here she did some of her most important work. She began working on the first electronic digital computer. It was called the UNIVAC I.

Grace Says:

"If you do something once, people will call it an accident. If you do it twice, they call it a coincidence. But do it a third time and you've just proven a natural law!"

Hopper in the early 1960s

PROGRAMMING FOR THE PEOPLE

Hopper wanted computers to be easy to use. She also wanted a simple language for computer programming. Hopper created the first computer compiler. It was called A-0. The compiler translated symbols into codes. Next, she created the FLOW-MATIC program. It used English phrases instead of symbols. People could use it more easily.

Computer programmers spent a lot of hours copying codes. So Hopper encouraged the people at her company to store their codes on a shared library.

Hopper is seen here working with UNIVAC.

Next, Hopper went to work on another new computer language. It is called COBOL. It stands for common business-oriented language. It was a computer language that was meant to be used for business. Many others also worked on COBOL. Hopper did a lot of work to let people know about COBOL. By the 1970s, COBOL was the most popular computer language in the world.

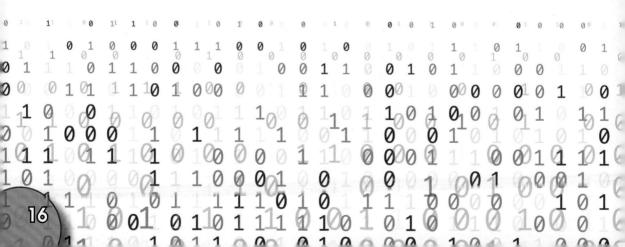

CHAPTER 4
BACK TO ACTIVE

In 1966, Hopper retired from the Navy. She said it was "the saddest day of my life." But she wasn't sad for long. The next year she went back to work. This time she was in charge of overseeing the computer languages. She had only planned on staying for six months. She stayed for nineteen years!

Hopper finally retired at the age of seventy-nine. She was the oldest officer serving in the American armed forces at the time! Hopper was also the first woman to reach the rank of **rear admiral**. She continued to help out with projects for the rest of her life.

Hopper had excellent writing skills. Hopper wrote the first computer programming manual.

Hopper in her office in the early 1980s.

The USS *Hopper* sails into the harbor in Sydney, Australia. The warship was named for Hopper in 1997.

"MAN" OF THE YEAR

Hopper received many awards and honors. In 1969, the Data Processing Management Association offered a new award. Hopper was the first to receive it. She also won the first computer sciences Man of the Year Award! In 1991, she won American's top technology award. President

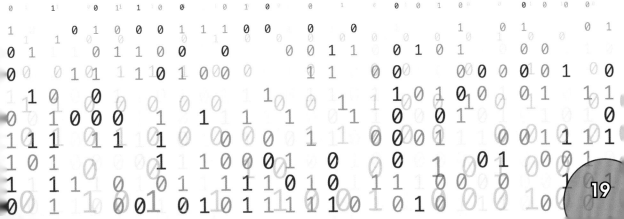

Hopper is saluted by sailors as she arrives at her retirement ceremony in 1986.

George H. W. Bush presented her with the National Medal of Technology. She was the first individual woman to receive it! She died January 1, 1992. The Navy named a warship after her. It is called the USS *Hopper*.

Grace Hopper once said, "I've come to feel that there is no use doing anything unless you can communicate." Her vision made computers much easier to use. She supported and taught others who worked in her field. And thanks to Hopper, computers are used by more people than ever, all over the world.

Grace Says:

"The most important thing I've accomplished, other than building the compiler, is training young people. They come to me...and say, 'Do you think we can do this?' I say 'Try it' and I back them up."

TIMELINE

1906 Grace Brewster Murray is born on December 9 in New York.

1928 Graduates from Vassar College.

1934 Earns her doctorate from Yale.

1941 Becomes a professor of math and physics at Vassar College.

1943 Joins the US Navy.

1947 Solves a computer problem when discovering a moth in it. She begins using the term "computer bug."

1949 Becomes senior mathematician at Eckert-Mauchly Computer Corporation.

1967 The Navy recalls Hopper to active duty.

1986 Final retirement from the Navy.

1992 Grace Murray Hopper dies on January 1.

2016 Is awarded the Presidential Medal of Freedom for her work in computer science.

2017 Yale University renames one of its colleges after Hopper.

LEARN MORE

BOOKS

Diehn, Andi. *Technology: Cool Women Who Code.* White River Junction, VT: Nomad Press, 2015.

Pelleschi, Andrea. *Mathematician and Computer Scientist Grace Hopper.* Minneapolis, MN: Lerner Publications, 2017.

Wallmark, Laurie. *Grace Hopper: Queen of Computer Code.* New York, NY: Sterling, 2017.

WEBSITES

Academic Kids

techagekids.com/2015/12/grace-hopper-computer-pioneer.html
Check out facts, a timeline, and more Hopper quotes.

***Beanz*: The Magazine for Kids, Code, and Computer Science**

kidscodecs.com/grace-hopper
Learn more about Hopper and her work.

INDEX

A
awards and honors, 19–21

B
"bug," 9
Bush, George H. W., 21

C
childhood, 5–7
COBOL, 16
computer compiler, 14

F
family, 5–6

FLOW-MATIC, 14

H
Harvard University, 9, 12

M
Mark I, 9–10
marriage and divorce, 7, 8
mathematician, 5, 12

N
nicknames, 5

P
programmer, 10, 14–16, 17

U
UNIVAC 1, 12
US Navy, 8–9, 12, 17
USS *Hopper*, 21

V
Vassar College, 7, 8

Y
Yale University, 7

Published in 2019 by Enslow Publishing, LLC.
101 W. 23rd Street, Suite 240, New York, NY 10011

Library of Congress Cataloging-in-Publication Data

Names: Niver, Heather Moore, author.
Title: Grace Hopper : computer scientist and navy admiral / Heather Moore Niver.
Description: New York : Enslow Publishing, 2019. | Series: Junior Biographies
| Audience: Grades 3-5. | Includes bibliographical references and index.
Identifiers: LCCN 2018008785| ISBN 9781978502048 (library bound) | ISBN
9781978502970 (pbk.) | ISBN 9781978502987 (6 pack)
Subjects: LCSH: Hopper, Grace Murray—Juvenile literature. | Admirals—United
States—Biography—Juvenile literature. | Computer engineers—United
States—Biography—Juvenile literature. | United States. Navy—Biography—Juvenile literature.
Classification: LCC V63.H66 N58 2019 | DDC 359.0092 [B] —dc23
LC record available at https://lccn.loc.gov/2018008785

Printed in the United States of America

Photos Credits: Cover, pp. 1, 18 Cynthia Johnson/The LIFE Images Collection/Getty Images; pp. 2, 3, 22, 23, 24, back cover (curves graphic) Alena Kazlouskaya/Shutterstock.com; p. 4 PJF Military Collection/Alamy Stock Photo; pp. 6, 11 Bettmann/Getty Images; pp. 8, 19, 20 © AP Images; p. 13 Interim Archives/Archive Photos/Getty Images; p. 15 Science Source/Getty Images; interior page bottoms (binary code) Ink Drop/Shutterstock.com.